Stronger Than Salmon

poems by

Carol Shamon

Finishing Line Press
Georgetown, Kentucky

Stronger Than Salmon

Copyright © 2024 by Carol Shamon
ISBN 979-8-88838-672-9 First Edition
All rights reserved under International and Pan-American Copyright Conventions. No part of this book may be reproduced in any manner whatsoever without written permission from the publisher, except in the case of brief quotations embodied in critical articles and reviews.

ACKNOWLEDGMENTS

"You Bring Out The Moon In Me" and "Home" appeared in *Relevant Poetry* First edition printed in February, 2022 Irrelevant Press

Publisher: Leah Huete de Maines
Editor: Christen Kincaid
Cover Art: Carol Shamon
Author Photo: Matt Furman
Cover Design: Elizabeth Maines McCleavy

Order online: www.finishinglinepress.com
also available on amazon.com

Author inquiries and mail orders:
Finishing Line Press
PO Box 1626
Georgetown, Kentucky 40324
USA

Contents

The Key 1

I Never Told Anyone 3

Green Blanket 4

New thought 5

Jesse 6

Bette 7

My Marriage Needs Mending 8

Home 9

Dear Children 10

You Bring Out the Moon In Me 11

Morning Coffee With My 92-Year-Old Mom 13

For Lynne 14

Light Magic 16

For David

The Key

I wake up writing poetry as fast as I can think
I'm lying stiff and blue
The key the key
All I'm missing is the key
Or maybe it's a hook behind me and my shirt is caught
And I'm running in place
All it takes is an easy unhooking
And no more running
Just skating and swimming, floating
Rising like the sun
Going to sleep in the dirt
Breathing lavender with every inhale

I'm told to ask
And I ask
I scan my dreams
Empty out my memories
A pile of dead boys
I search for the hand reaching out still
My womb still empty
After 66 tries
Three babies
And countless moons and tides and words
Words

In the harsh light
I peek at my silver hair
Surprised
Because my heart is still so new
It's soft
Is just being born
Again and again
Every night
Over and over

Red and purple and alive
In the stiff blue body
It swallows the words
The keys
The hooks
It's a baby with a hungry mouth
It doesn't know about angels
Or mistakes
The dirt and the sky are the same

And now I must walk around inside out
The hook still stuck behind me
Keyless clueless
My slippery heart
Dripping, leaking
I'd choose dirt over words
If I could

I Never Told Anyone

About the night it snowed enough to give the streets a thick coating
And all the neighborhood kids got to go sledding down
The Newport hill without parents
White flakes billowing from the streetlights
Us bundled up
red cheeks cold noses
A whole gang of us
Feeling the joy of the fast ride down the hill
until the metal runners slowed
scraping the pavement

One boy had dragged his foot on the fresh snowy slope of a yard
and wrote a message
The way lovers do on the beach in the sand
I trudged over in my snow clumped boots to read it
Dirty Jew was what he wrote
And the red from my cheeks went inward and my whole head felt hot
as I walked home
alone

Green Blanket

You wrapped in a green blanket
The sky turning color and then gray

You say
that I have things I keep in my cape
that I bring out when you are ready

I say
I am spider web lost
the connections are too thin

We both feel the dance wind
We feel our hearts getting bigger

My fear is just under
the next page

My Dr. says
"clear your harbor"

I fumble around
Organize my poems and paintings
I'll try a new room

We have a casual conversation on the phone
I know the blanket and the cape
are folded
The sky turns
magnificent colors anyway

New Thought

Woke with
The thought
Of a new love
Not withheld
A tiny crack in my shell
The golden light could warm me

Realizing the moon wakes me
Whatever bed I'm in

Driving
Through Jacaranda streets
The sky gray
Purples pop and float
Everywhere
Around us
Between us

On the precipice of porch
Hope surrounds us like air
The sun leaving
The birds calling
The hillside pregnant
With dance and fires
Leaves to caress
Grapes to burst
Words and silence
A deep breath
A new thought

Jesse

Jesse is lost
We can't find him
When it's this quiet
He is in jail or hospital
Or maybe tucked up under an angel's wing

He's lost to us in different ways
Swept under the carpet
Put in the back of the spare closet
With the old pictures and the BB gun

They forgot
The earnestness
The politeness
The glue

I wish I could find him again
Put my hand on his forehead
And see all those smiles
The wicked one
The sweet one
The sarcastic one
And the sad one

Bette

Your dead mother is coming back
Your insane and truthful brother sends photos
Over email
Photos that never dreamed of traveling such a way

It's before she couldn't speak
When she was tall and proud and thought she might be happy

Our young feminist daughter dreams of her
In the dream she is helping her grandmother to stand up

She comes to my dreams too
We are naked together and realize we are the same
I say it is good we have found this new place
She begins to look sleeker, healthier

In the same dream I realize that I have not been walking tall
I tell myself that I need to remember all I am
The things yet to be done floating ahead of me
Life preservers

My Marriage Needs Mending

My marriage needs mending
I'm sewing it with a needle
With no thread
It is silently ending

I try strapping on huge wings
Of possibility
I can do it for moments

My secrets have changed
To truth
They never needed to spill

Home

My soul knows the geography, the topography
But it is miles and miles
Before my body can locate it
Steppingstone path of soft hearts

Sometimes I hammer blindfolded
Using my own bones for nails
I climb the scaffolding that I've left up
Just to feel the breeze
That's always been there

No screens on the open windows
I want to feel the same inside
As I do outside
The coyotes are here too
And can step through the sash at any time

I battled for this home
Scraped layers of barnacles from the walls
Removed scar tissue that had grown like ropes
Over the key holes

Truth grows in the courtyard garden
Spreads under the cracks beneath the doors
Lands like sun rays
On white sheets

Dear Children

I tried
in the mornings
serving you French toast made soft and warm
sweetened with so much butter and syrup
I thought you wouldn't notice
salty tears falling like crystals on the dishes
as I washed them

Sending
you out with all the checkmarks
lunches packed, hairs cut, homework done
then taking a quick breath behind the door
alone in my bathroom
hoping the world would join me
in doing the right thing
keeping you sturdy

At night
After I locked the front door
and tucked you in the beds
I didn't notice the cold breeze
Coming in under the back door
snaking up to your rooms
Swirling around your heads

Trying to fit into my own spot in the bed
and rebuild our house over and over again
I hope you will forget
when I wasn't in love
and the house would fall each night as we slept
I thought you wouldn't notice

You Bring Out the Moon in Me

*From the prompt You Bring Out the Mexican in Me
by Sandra Cisneros*

You bring out the moon in me
My first real baby to make it
In the midst of all my doubts
About myself
My great power
You arrive perfect
Separate
An orbit around me
A tiny powerful mouth
Sucking on my small breast
Attaching me and you to the moon
To ancient times
Doubtless times
When the moon was bigger
And night was part of day
Not the collapse
The door closing

You bring out the moon in me
You need me
You demand me
You command me
You sing and dance me
You scream me
You take me to the edge
And then sleep in bliss
With wet thumb falling out of open mouth
I sleep with one eye open

You bring out the moon in me
The wonder
The secrets
The knowing
The showing

The tears
And the trying
The lostness
The Cinderella romance

You standing so tall
And spewing the truth
You cutting your hair
You walking away
You afraid of night
Fearing the moon you have brought

You bring out the moon in me
We cycle together
I dream that your tiny nose
Has become like mine
My daughter
My sister
My mother
My opposite reflection
My eclipse

You bring the moon to me
We hold it together
We set it on the table between us
And we eat it
We dance fearless steps
Following the tide
We hold the moon in our bellies
And smile the smile of women
You me and the moon
An eternity of firsts
Of sadness
Of love
Between us

Morning Coffee with my 92 year old Mom

When I come to visit she always asks if I believe in life after death
I always tell her that I do and then she says that she wishes she did
but thinks there is nothing

Soon we slip into the stories
I've heard them many times
but never remind her of this

The stories are slivers that have pierced her and as she digs them out
they appear golden

When my father would bath us as babies
And mop the kitchen floor
His beautiful death
How she told her ancient Mother that of course her money had not run out
when of course it had years before
Her fat, stern uncle who turned out to be so kind and so wise
The one and only time she felt anger toward her Mother-in-law
Her Grandfather the rabbi stroking his long beard, her Grandmother
with her head covered, washing clothes with a washboard

Each story is a door
Those we have loved and sometimes feared
silently enter and rise like the glittering dust

The sunlit room with only our two voices
becomes a sanctuary
no mourner's candles are needed

For Lynne (My Sister)

Today is your birthday
You would have been 70 today
It's been 7 years since you died

I made sure to have my coffee from the hand painted Italian cup
You gave to me
Probably 40 years ago

Of course you never imagined the cup
Would become my link to you
That on mornings I choose my Lynne cup
I give the cold ceramic side of it a kiss
And whisper warm words to you

When you sent me a birthday card two months before your death
I believe that you knew that card would link us
You wrote in your lovely script only these words
"I carry your heart—I carry it in my heart"
From an E.E. Cummings poem

It was you who took my own poetry seriously
Well, you took me seriously and encouraged me to study at Naropa
I did. I went to your Boulder CO and tested myself, my words

I see you now in glimpses
Mostly from your days in your big bed you called the boat
From the boat you could still watch the news
And you could still be funny
Until the window started to shrink and became just a pin hole

But you were still sneaky
Walking yourself to the bathroom when I told you to ask me for help
I later wiped the pale excrement from your toes
That were turning blue
Hoping you wouldn't notice
That I noticed

I am here still
Two years older than you got be

I'm going to try to write poems again
Get back to the girl you saw me as
The girl I was going to be once

It's just a cup I've had for a long time
It will eventually crack or chip
It's ok if it does
I carry your heart (I carry it in my heart)

Light Magic

Late at night
I follow the quiet
illuminated terraced rectangles
traveling around the walls of my bedroom

One at a time
each wall is blessed
The room becomes sacred
as the light rolls by in tandem
with the ordinary car
driving down the street

When my son was a toddler
strapped in his car seat
looking out the back window
He solemnly informed me
"I can make the sun turn blue"
Did he do it by squinting his eyes?
No matter
I smiled at his super power

My partners' late wife Linda
Loved pink light bulbs
We still have a few left
When we click on the antique lamp
and sit in the soft pink glow
We invite Linda in the room
to join us

When I close my eyes and look
I see a moving map of light and color
Bright beacons pointing
to my soul's preference
The light like stars within
Sanctifying my place
In the outer world

Carol Shamon is a writer and painter living in San Diego, CA. She's been a journal keeper and poet for most of her life. While in college she contributed to several publications including *Colorado-North Review* and *Poetry-North Review*. After college she attended the Jack Kerouac School of Disembodied Poetics for two summers studying poetry with Allen Ginsberg and Anne Waldman.

Her most recent poetry publications include the UK magazine *Seedlings*, The online publications *Spillwords* and *RedRoseThorns*, and the 2024 San Diego Poets Annual. She was an honorable mention in the 2023 *Ocean-Earth-Air Art and Poetry* book. She had three poems in the December 2023 issue of *Summation*. In 2022 she had two poems published in the book *Relevant Poetry* published by Irrelevant Press as well as two poems in the 2022 issue of *Summation*.

In 2020 Irrelevant Press published her zine *A Different More* Creating and Embracing Change While Aging. The zine *Oh The Water* was published the summer of 2023. She is currently working on her memoir *The Decade House*.

In what feels like another lifetime ago, she created and owned the successful Shamon Freitas talent agency for 35 years. She is the proud mama of three wonderful children, and the grandmother of Audra. She lives in San Diego with her loving partner Dave.

www.ingramcontent.com/pod-product-compliance
Lightning Source LLC
Chambersburg PA
CBHW031222100426
PP18119500001B/1